TEMPLAR, ARIZONA.

1 - The Great Outdoors.

By Spike.

www.TemplarAZ.com

WWW.IRONCIRCUS .COM

This volume collects the first chapter of Templar, Arizona.
More of the story is available at http://www.templaraz.com.

Write Spike: ironcircus@gmail.com

First Edition: May 2007
Second Edition: February 2009

ISBN: 978-0-9794080-0-7

Printed in Canada

1 – The Great Outdoors.

YOU **SWORE**. I **HEARD** YOU.

I DIDN'T.

FUCK YOU. YOU **DID**. BUT I'M NOT GOING TO PRESS IT. BECAUSE I DON'T **CARE** THAT YOU DID. I COULDN'T POSSIBLY CARE **LESS** ABOUT WHAT YOU THINK. ABOUT **ANYTHING**.

GOOD MORNING, MR. PIERCE.

I DON'T CONSIDER YOUR OPINIONS **WORTHY** OF RECOGNITION BEYOND THAT WHICH MY EMPLOYER AND YOURS **FORCE** ME TO ALLOW FOR.

I MAY CHANGE MY MIND WHEN YOU ACHIEVE A **MULTISYLLABIC VOCABULARY**, BUT I FIND MYSELF QUITE SKEPTICAL OF THAT.

SCRATCH SCRATCH MUSS COMB

YOU GIVE ME THE IMPRESSION OF AN ANIMAL. A SMALL, **POINTLESS** ANIMAL. SOMETHING LIKE A **SHREW**.

OKAY.

IN BETTER TIMES, YOU WOULD HAVE BEEN FED TO **PIGS**. AND **I** WOULD HAVE **EATEN** THOSE PIGS.

UM.

BUT APPARENTLY, MY LONG, GRUELING, THOROUGHLY UNREWARDING YEARS EDITING DISTINCTIVE AND AWARD-WINNING METROPOLITAN NEWSPAPERS DON'T COUNT FOR ANYTHING, BECAUSE I CAN BE OVERRULED BY A MOB OF POMPOUS, ILLITERATE ART FAGS WHO HAVE NEVER READ ANYTHING MORE COMPLEX THAN HOP ON POP.
SO THE NEW JOB'S YOURS. GOD HELP US ALL.
JOB?

JOB. THE TOPIC OF THIS PHONE CALL, BENJAMIN.
I'LL BE NEEDING A BI-WEEKLY OPINION PIECE FROM YOU IN ADDITION TO WEDNESDAY'S COLUMNS. FREE TOPIC, INFORMAL TONE, ONE THOUSAND WORDS. SLIGHT BUMP IN PAY.

OH.
OKAY. YES. YES, SIR. THANK YOU, S-
YOU'RE NOT GONZO, ARE YOU?

NO SIR, I'M NOT.
FUCKING GONZO. I DON'T PAY YOU TO GET STONED AND WRITE ABOUT IT, YOU UNDERSTAND ME?

IF YOU **EVER** HAND ME SOME FUCKING TRAVESTY ABOUT PEYOTE AND QUAALUDES AND MEXICAN TRANSVESTITES, I WILL **STRANGLE** YOU LIKE A GODDAMMITIN' **PARAKEET.**

I WILL TWIST YOUR HEAD **OFF. CLEAN. OFF.**

SNIFF.

AND I WILL DO IT OVER THE **PHONE.**

EVERYONE WILL BE **AMAZED.**

I'M SURE THEY WILL, SIR.

UNSCREW
UNSCREW.

GL'IG.

— FROM YOUR OWN PUCKERED ASSHOLE. I SWEAR TO GOD AND CHRIST HIMSELF.
UH-HUH.
PICKLES

SEE. I WOULDN'T KNOW IF YOU WERE GONZO OR NOT. I DON'T READ YOUR COLUMN.
YOUR WORK IS COMPLETELY IMPENETRABLE. I CAN'T DECIPHER IDIOT.
PTP.

IT'S ATTRACTIVE TO BELIEVE THAT YOU WERE MADE IN HELL, AND SENT EXCLUSIVELY TO TORMENT ME.
IT APPEALS TO MY EGO.
BUT I HAVE NEVER DONE ANYTHING FOUL ENOUGH TO DESERVE SOMETHING LIKE YOU.
SCRAPE SCRAPE.
DELI

WOULD YOU LIKE TO HEAR A SECRET, BENJAMIN?
YOU'D LIKE IT. IT'S WORTHLESS.
HM?
MUNCH MUNCH MUNCH.

I'M GOING TO KILL MYSELF.
RUSTLE RUSTLE.
SOON.

AND I AM GOING TO MAKE IT LOOK LIKE MURDER.
MURDER COMMITTED BY ONE OF YOU GODFORSAKEN MOUTHBREATHERS.

AND WHEN YOU'RE IN JAIL FOR MY MURDER, I AM GOING TO HAUNT YOU. RELENTLESSLY.
THAT'S...
...
I HOPE THAT WORKS OUT FOR YOU, SIR.

NO YOU DON'T.
LEAVING NOW.

...
BYE..?
RUSTLE.
DRAG.

YANK.

ZORA.
TUG.
TUG.

ZORADYSIS.
HI.

YEAH, HI.
HEY, ZORA, WHERE'S REAGAN?
GO FIND REAGAN.

NO THANK YOU.
YOU DON'T HAVE SOME PANTS, BENJAMIN.

AOH.
CHECK THE HAMPER.
HELP FOLD.
UHM.
SHOW ME HOW.
SPEED DIAL.

RING. RING.
FIVE.
FIVE SHIRTS, OKAY? AND SOCKS.
OKAY, BEN?
UH-HUH.

PICK UP.
PICK UP, RAY.
RING. RING. RING.
AND THEN MAYBE PANTS, BEN?
OKAY?
ha.

got you again.
but i lost you though, huh.
can't keep doin' that.

WHAT.
YEEE!

DADDY!
DADDY
DADDY
whoops.
hi.
DADDY
yeah.
what.

huh. oh.
yeah. okay.
i got told about you.
KISS
KISS
KISS.

REALLY? HEH.
WOW.

TOTAL SILENCE.

ben.
YES!

not you. him.
YES, DADDY!

i'm gene.
i'm over you.
ow.
can you hear me?

. . .
WHAT?
IN YOUR APARTMENT?
THROUGH THE CEILING, YOU MEAN?
I... DUNNO. I, I GUESS SO. DO YOU OWN A GUITAR?

this is my zora.
WE'VE MET.
she was in the tub.
she got away.

RIGHT.
BEN GAVE ME SHIRTS.
cool.
MUTHERACHRIST JESUS YOU HAVE GOT T'BE KIDDING ME.

OH. NICE.
YOU JUST GOTTA MAKE ME TH' BAD GUY T'DAY, DON'TCHA.
GOD DAMN, GENE.
whoops.

YEAH, I ONLY GOT OFF LIKE MAYBE TWENTY MINUTES AGO.
FUCKIN' GRAVE SHIFT RELIEF BETTER BE DEAD INNA GADDAM DITCH.
SHOULDA NARC'ED HIS ASS OUT TH' FIRST TIME.
we're not going.
KNOCK IT OFF, GENE.
she's sick.
I COUGHED.
i heard her.
she'll go tomorrow.
SHE'LL GO NOW.
GENE, ZORA'S NOT MISSING HER FIRST DAY OF SCHOOL.
THAT'S JUST FUCKIN' RETARDED.
PEOPLE ARE GONNA NOTICE THAT, OKAY?

SO THIS AIN'T UP FOR DISCUSSION.
G'WAN UPSTAIRS. I'M COMIN' FOR TH' BOTH-A YOU IN TEN MINUTES. SHE'S GETTIN' WALKED T'CLASS, WHETHER SHE'S READY OR NOT.
AND I MEAN IT. SO SAY OKAY.
okay.

I —
I THINK THIS IS YOURS.
no.
my clothes are bigger.
that's zora's.

NO IT'S NOT.

LEAVE.

SIGH.

AN' YER JUST GONNA LET HER WALK RIGHT OUT TH' DOOR WITH HALF-A YER GADDAM CLOTHES ON, AREN'TCHA.
GOD.
I CAN GET THEM LATER.
I GUESS.
IT'S OKAY.

GET 'EM NOW, DUMMY. YOU CAN STILL CATCH 'EM.
NO.
NAH. I'M FINE. IT'S FINE.
I'VE GOT A FEW LEFT.
THIS ONE'S PRETTY CLEAN.
JEE-! ZIZ!
EVERYBODY UP IN YAKIMA AS PUSSY AS YOU, BENNY?
EVERYONE IN YAKIMA HAS A FRONT DOOR THAT LOCKS.

HAW.
WASSAMATTER, YOU DON'T TRUST PEOPLE? CUZ YOU GOT NUTHIN' I WANT, SUBURBS.
I'D JUST PREFER A WORKING DOOR.
YOUR DOOR WORKS. I'LL BET EVERYONE ELSE'S DOORS WORK.
I DIDN'T EVEN HEAR ZORA GET IN, TODAY. SHE COULD HAVE SEEN ME NAKED.

HE DIDN'T LIKE ZORA, EITHER.
I LIKE ZORA OKAY.
YEAH?
THAT WHY YOU'RE SO COOL WITH HER JACKIN' ALL YER SHIT? CUZ I CAN LET HER KNOW.

I TRY NOT TO FORCIBLY STRIP LITTLE GIRLS IN FRONT OF THEIR PARENTS IF I CAN HELP IT, REAGAN.
PLEASE.
LIKE GENE WOULD EVEN KNOW IT'S WRONG.

UHM. YEAH.
SO, UH, ABOUT GENE? MAYBE IT'S JUST ME, BUT—
OOOoH.
OH. OH MAN I LOVE IT WHEN YOU GET ALL TACTFUL LIKE THAT.
GO ON. ASK. I'LL TELL YOU.

...I DON'T REALLY KNOW HOW TO PUT IT.
WIPE.
HE WASN'T LIT UP, IF THAT'S WHAT'CHER THINKIN'.
THAT WAS ALL GENE, THERE.
HE'S JUST STUPID.

OH.
NOT REALLY BADLY STUPID.
NOT HELMET-ALL-THE-TIME STUPID.
BUT, Y'KNOW. HE MESSES UP, HERE AN' THERE.
GETS BY OKAY, THOUGH.

HELL, PROB'LY DOES BETTER'N ME. HALF TH' TIME YOU SEEN ME BABYSITTIN' ZORA'S CUZ HE'S GOT A GIG.
HE'S IN A BAND, IF YOU CAN BELIEVE THAT SHIT. A REAL ONE. LIKE, FOR A LIVING. YOU EVER BEEN ACROSS TH' RIVER TO BESSIE STRONG'S?
NO.
TOO BAD. YOU SHOULD GO, THEY'RE REGULARS THERE.
HOW ABOUT BRAZENHEAD? DOWN ON REGENCY?
TAP TAP.

UH-UH.
WELL, Y'KNOW THEY PLAY SPACEGRASS TOO, RIGHT? GENE CAN GET US IN.
BAND'S CALLED BORNDOWN. ONE WORD. FUCKIN' HIPSTERS LOVE EM'.
WHERE'S SPACEGRASS?

...
CHRIST, BENNY. IT'S TWO BLOCKS UP.
YOU CAN SEE IT FROM TH' STOOP.
YOU NEVER EVEN WALKED BY?
I DON'T REALLY GET OUT MUCH.

RIGHT.
I GUESS I WORK A LOT. THE PAPER'S KIND OF DEMANDING.
UH-HUH.

AND I **THINK** I GOT A PROMOTION THIS MORNING, TOO. BUT IT'S KINDA HARD TO TELL. MY EDITOR'S A LITTLE, UH...
yeah.
SO, Y'KNOW. STUFF.

STUFF.
mostly.

GOOD **LORD.**
GET DRESSED.
I AM DRESSED.
REAL CLOTHES.
YER GOIN' OUTSIDE.
NOW.
TODAY.

I DO
SHH.
SHH. NO, MY KITTEN. NO. THIS IS WRONG.
THAT IS A FACT.
TWO MONTHS IN TOWN AN' YOU'D GET LOST TAKIN' A PISS.
I CANNOT ABIDE THIS.

YOU AN' ME, WE'LL GO WALKIN', ALL RIGHT? IT'LL BE FUN. WE'LL GO T'KING STREET. YOU LIKE KING STREET?
SHIT, I BET YOU NEVER EVEN BEEN.
THAT'S... REALLY...
REAGAN, I APPRECIATE THE OFFER, BUT IT'S NOT—
I GOTTA GO RUN ZORA AN' GENE T'SCHOOL, BUT I'LL BE BACK INNA HALF HOUR.
YOU BE READY, OKAY?
WEAR SUMTHIN' THAT'LL MAKE TH' TOURISTS NERVOUS.
REAGAN, I CAN'T.

I'M NOT GOING.
I DON'T WANT TO.
WELL SHIT, I KNOW THAT.
WHY D'YOU THINK I'M MAKIN' YA?

THE
OARLOCK
24-7
LOVE OVER THE
RIVER
DAILY
KING STREET
SHUTTLES
IT'S A MIRACLE
NO ONE'S BEEN
KILLED
—IN THE—
COLISEUM
WITH
CLAUDIUS R. GRAVES
CHANNEL
21·A
FLATWORM
SHINER
BEAUTIFUL
DAMAGE

...PETRIFIED DEER PENIS, WITH SESAME AND LEMON.
FRUIT BAT CONSOMMÉ.

MINERVA'S SHIELD... THAT'S MOSTLY PIKE LIVERS, LARK TONGUES, AND SOME PEACOCK BRAIN...
FOREVER
TRUE
STIR-FRIED PORPOISE HEAD.

HONEY-GRILLED PANTHER WITH EARWIGS...
NOW
POLICE
MEAT IS

AND, OF COURSE, **PUPPIES.** WHOLE AND QUARTERS.
BRAISED, BROILED, OR GRILLED.
IN A DELICATE HUMAN MILK SAUCE. **EXCELLENT.**
XENOPHAGE
MORALLY INDEFENSIBLE FINE DINING

XENOPHAGE
THANK YOU.
THANKS SO MUCH.

YOU KNOW, I REALLY **ENJOY** THESE LITTLE GET-TOGETHERS WE HAVE.
AND I SUSPECT YOU DO, TOO.
SAME TIME TOMORROW, THEN?
POLICE LINE DO NOT CROSS

THE SASSY CAVY

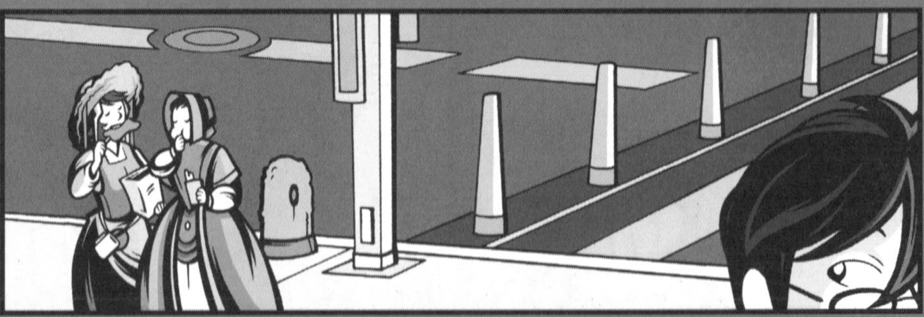

hmn.
YOU GOT A **PEN NAME** OR SUMTHIN? CUZ I'M NOT SEEIN' ANY BENJAMIN KOWALSKI IN HERE.
CHECK THE BACK, PAST THE BROTHEL ADS.
MAD MONK ALE
THE TEMPLAR CRUSADE
HEY, ARE THOSE **PASTIMES?**

YEAH, RIGHT. GOD FORBID TH' RESTA US BE SPARED TH' FUCKIN' FASHION SHOW.
C'MON. DON'T LET 'EM CATCH YA STARIN', THEY'LL COME OVER'N DO LATIN AT YA.
REALLY?
I'VE NEVER SEEN ANY BEFORE.

YOU GOTTA LEAVE TH' BUILDING MORE OFTEN.

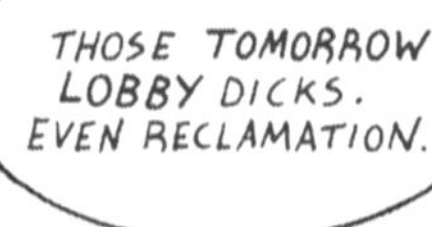
PLENTY-A CHANCES T'GET SICK OF 'EM IN THIS PART-A TOWN.
YOU DON'T LIKE PASTIMES?

I DON'T DIG ON ANY-A TH' DIPSHIT KING STREET CIRCLE JERKS PEOPLE GOT GOIN'.
PASTIMES. SINCERISTS.

THOSE TOMORROW LOBBY DICKS. EVEN RECLAMATION.
I NEVER SEEN SO MANY PEOPLE WORK SO HARD AT BEIN' SO FUCKIN' STUPID.

YOU GONNA COME DOWN BY TH' RIVER, THERE'S BETTER SHIT'N THAT T'LOOK AT.
EXAMPLE.
oh.
oh, okay.

huh.

HUH.

wuh.
WAIT.
NO.
OH, BUT YES.
NO.
HAW HAW.

CALDONIA'S
WELCOME T'TEMPLAR, NEW BOY.
CARTER

BUT THEN TH' NAVAJO GOT ALL CRAZY AND PISSED OFF IN THE SEVENTIES, RIGHT?

WANTED THE THING TOOK DOWN.

BUT TH' CITY COUNCIL, THEY DIN'T WANNA LOSE A WHOLE STATUE.

SO THEY JUST JACKHAMMERED OFF ALL THE INDIAN HEADS.

AN' NOW JACKSON'S JUST BASHIN' TH' SHIT OUTTA A BUNCHA HEADLESS DUDES IN LOINCLOTHS.

AND IT'S LIKE A MILLION TIMES WORSE.

BEAUTIFUL.

C'MON, KEEP WALKIN'. WE AIN'T EVEN GOTTEN STARTED.
TURN IN HERE.
WHERE ARE WE GOING?
FIRST STOP. CUTE JOINT I KNOW. KINDA OFF TH' MAIN DRAG, SO IT STAYS HALFWAY DECENT WITH TH' LOW PEOPLE.
KING STREET'S BETTER WHEN Y'GOTTA BUZZ ON. WE KIN GET A CHEAP PITCHER.
DRINKING BEFORE NOON?
BEER AIN'T DRINKIN'.

SO, IT'S LIKE...
I MEAN...
CROSS-EYED MARY'S
CLAY BAR
EST. 1984
HE'S NOT A BAD PERSON.
IT'S KINDA HARD TO EXPLAIN. AND I WAS SLEEPING? SO MAYBE I MADE IT WORSE.
HE WAS AT WORK AT SEVEN. BUT I SLEEP DURING THE DAY, SO... YOU KNOW.

I'D HEARD ABOUT HIM FROM OTHER CRUSADE WRITERS. BUT I FIGURED...
"HEY, LET'S SCARE THE NEW GUY."
"EVIL EDITOR STORYTIME."
BUT PIERCE IS JUST...
IF LOATHING COULD DIAL A PHONE.
SO WHAT'D YOU SAY?

HUH?
WHEN HE WAS TALKIN' ALL HIS SHIT. PIGS N' GHOSTS N' WHATEVER.
WHAT DID YOU SAY BACK?
I
I DON'T
HE DOESN'T REALLY LET YOU.
SO NUTHIN.'
HUH. DAMN.
YOU FAILED.
FAILED WHAT?
THE TEST, BEN.
WHAT, YOU DUNNO WHEN YOU'RE GETTIN' FUCKED WITH?
YOU GOTTA GET BORN, KIDDO.
IT WASN'T - IT'S NOT LIKE THAT. HE DOES IT TO EVERYONE.
BET NOT. BET HE JUST KNOWS WHO'LL ROLL OVER FOR IT.
NO, I MEAN IT. HE'S ALWAYS BEEN THAT WAY.
THEN YOU FAILED A LONG TIME AGO.
YOU SEE WHAT I'M SAYIN,' RIGHT?
HE KNOWS YOU'LL TAKE IT.
OH. YEAH.
OK.
sorry.

YEAH, GIMME A BLACK COFFEE. BRING TH' POT.

SURE.

Y'WANNA **MONK** OR SUMTHIN', BENNY? I'M BUYIN'.

OH. I THOUGHT THE BEER WAS GONNA BE FOR YOU.

I DON'T DRINK.

HOW ABOUT A **CHIMERA**, THEN?

OKAY.

...AND HE DOESN'T DRINK.
JEE-ZIZ LORD.
GROPE.
I GUESS IT'S TOO MUCH T'HOPE THAT'S CUZ YOU GOT ALL FUCKED UP ONE TIME AN' KILLED A BUNCHA DUDES, HUH?
I'M KINDA BORING.

YEAH, NO SHIT.
YOU SURE YOU'RE A WRITER?
NOT REALLY.
HA!
SLAP.
WELL, IF THAT GREAT AMERICAN NOVEL DON'T WORK OUT, LEMME KNOW. I DO MOSTA TH' HIRING DOWN AT TH' SHOP.

IT AIN'T AS BAD AS MOST RETAIL. Y'DON'T EVEN GOTTA BE POLITE.
MAYBE. I'M PROBABLY NOT QUALIFIED, THOUGH.
I BET I'D NEED A DIPLOMA.

TH' HELL YOU DO.
Y'THINK I WENT T'COLLEGE?
I MEANT A HIGH SCHOOL DIPLOMA.
WELL. N'HERE I THOUGHT I HAD YOU PEGGED.
HOWJA MANAGE THAT?
I, UHM, I STOPPED GOING. SENIOR YEAR.
JUST STOPPED.
JUST STOPPED.
GOD. YOU ARE SO CUTE.
THANK YOU.
SO THAT'S TH' STORY. YOU MOVED A MILLION MILES T'BLOW OFF SCHOOL.
NO. I'M TWENTY-ONE. THAT WAS YEARS AGO.
THEN WHY'D Y'DITCH WASHINGTON? Y'LOOKIN' FOR SUMTHIN' T'WRITE ABOUT?
I GUESS.

I DON'T REALLY KNOW WHAT I'M DOING.
NOBODY DOES.
WELL, YEAH. MAYBE. PROBABLY. BUT I DON'T REALLY MEAN IT LIKE THAT.
I MEAN, IT'S **WEIRD** THAT I'M DOING THIS. WRITING. BEING A **WRITER**.

I GOT NO FUCKIN' IDEA WHAT YOU'RE TALKIN' ABOUT.
OH. OKAY.
okay. uh.

ALRIGHT. IT'S KINDA LIKE THIS.
WHEN I SENT THE CRUSADE MY SAMPLES, AND THEY SAID THEY WOULD PUBLISH ME...

... I WAS LUCKY. I KNOW I GOT LUCKY.
NO PROFESSIONAL EXPERIENCE. NO DEGREE. NO ANYTHING.
THEY DIDN'T HAVE TO TAKE ME. THEY PROBABLY SHOULDN'T HAVE, BUT THEY DID.

SO I THOUGHT, "OKAY. I GOT LUCKY."
"TIME TO BE SERIOUS. ACT LIKE A WRITER."
AND WRITERS READ, RIGHT?
REAL BOOKS. THE CLASSICS. SO I GOT SOME.
GREAT EXPECTATIONS, PRIDE AND PREJUDICE, AND ROBINSON CRUSOE.
AND, UH.
YEAH, THEY WERE TERRIBLE.

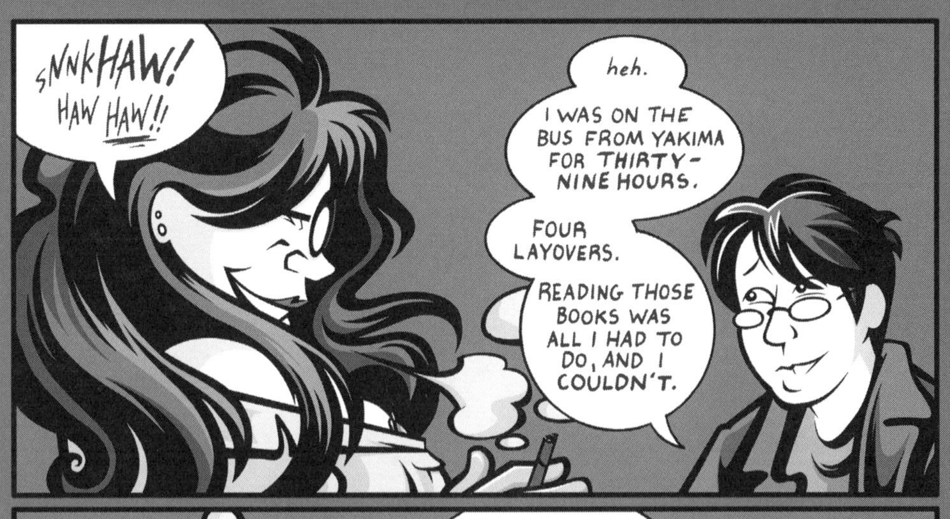

SNNKHAW!
HAW HAW!!
heh.
I WAS ON THE BUS FROM YAKIMA FOR THIRTY-NINE HOURS.
FOUR LAYOVERS.
READING THOSE BOOKS WAS ALL I HAD TO DO, AND I COULDN'T.

IT WAS LIKE TRYING TO BREATHE GLUE.
I'VE NEVER FELT MORE SUBLITERATE IN MY ENTIRE LIFE.

AND I LIKE BOOKS. REALLY. I REALLY DO.
JUST... NOT THE RIGHT ONES, I GUESS.

JUST TH' WRONG ONES, HUH?
MM. KINDA.
I MEAN, I BASICALLY READ JUNK. GIMMICK BOOKS.
LIKE EMPIRE OF MICHAEL, THAT BACTERIUM'S-EYE-VIEW THING? I REALLY LIKED THAT ONE.
AND THAT ONE SERIES WHERE PEOPLE FIGURE OUT HOW TO TALK TO GOD, EXCEPT HE'S COMPLETELY AUTISTIC?
RED GREEN SEVENTEEN.
YEAH, I SEEN COMMERCIALS FER THAT.
UH-HUH. SO, UM.
GARBAGE.
SHIT, MAN, WE GOTTA FUCK NOW!
COPY BOOKS? YOU?!

okay.
coffee an' a chimera.
WHO D'YOU READ? WHERE D'YOU BUY?!
Y'MEAN REAL COPY BOOKS, RIGHT?

THERE ARE FAKE ONES?
AH, THEY SELL SHINY, MAGAZINE-LOOKIN' RAGS TO TH' POSEURS UP AN' DOWN THIS BLOCK.
CRAP FULLA BEER ADS N' STAFF PAGES.
PSHT.

ONE GUY. PHOTOCOPIER. STAPLER.
THAT'S A COPY BOOK. TH' REAL LOW PEOPLE SHIT.
STARTED OUT WITH TH' LOW PEOPLE TOO, Y'KNOW.
JUST LIKE EVERYTHING WORTHA DAMN IN THIS TOWN.

WHO WAS YOUR FIRST?
whisper it to me.
I CAN'T EVEN SAY.
THERE WERE SOME IN THE BUS STATION.
ONE MORE IN THE TAXI.

YEAH, PEOPLE TRY N' LEAVE 'EM FLOATIN' WHEN THEY'RE DONE.
GOOD MANNERS.
Ooo.
I HAD A WHOLE PILE BEFORE I EVEN FOUND MY APARTMENT.

TWO WERE BY THE SAME GUY.
"RADICAL ANTI-WASTE STRATEGIES."
LOTS OF ROADKILL RECIPES AND LINT-KNITTING TECHNIQUES.
ONE HAD POETRY. EVERY VERSE ENDED WITH "DOINK."
IT WAS ACTUALLY PRETTY GOOD.
AND, UHM, A, UH, A PORNO THING.

IT'S CALLED AMBER'S CONFESSIONS, BUT... YEAH, A GUY IS WRITING IT. DEFINITELY.
OH, INDEED.

THE STATE VS REAGAN MANCUSO EXHIBIT A
Y'KNOW WHAT Y'GOTTA DO NOW, RIGHT?
YOU GOTTA WRITE ONE, TOO. IT'S TH' RULES.

HA.
NO, NO.
HAVE TO. DON'T FUCK UP TH' ROTATION, DUDE.
NO, I DON'T THINK SO.
WHY NOT? **WRITE,** WRITER.

I DON'T HAVE ANYTHING TO SAY.
SO?
HALF TH' COPY BOOKS OUT THERE GOT NUTHIN' T'SAY.

I GOT A TWENTY-PAGER AT HOME ABOUT WHAT SOME GUY HAD FOR **BREAKFAST.**
THAT'S KINDA DIFFERENT.
YEAH, **YOU** DO **REAL** WRITING.
PEOPLE **PAY** YOU.
SO **YOU** PROBABLY KNOW WHAT TH' HELL YOU'RE **DOING.**

YOU'D **THINK** THAT.
eesh.
FINE. **BE** A PUSSY.
swear t' god.

SO GET STARTED ON YER CHIMERA.
WE GOT PLACES T'BE.

WHERE?
WE GOTTA COUPLE MORE HOURS T'KILL DOWNTOWN, BUT I WANNA GET BACK BY NOON.
SOMEBODY I WANT'CHA T'MEET.
I GOTTA GET TH' TWO-A YOU IN' TH' SAME ROOM.
SEE IF THAT MUCH **DORK** CAN EXIST IN ONE SPOT.

WHO IS IT?
NOSY.
HEY, GIMME.

AW.
SO SWEET.

STAB.

SQUEEZE
SQUISH
SCULPT.
uh.

AN' NOW THEY'RE FRIENDS.
CRAM.

JAIL FRIENDS.
SHOVE.

EMPEROR WU OF CHINA WAS A BENEVOLENT BUDDHIST.
HE BUILT TEMPLES AND MONESTARIES.
HE EDUCATED COUNTLESS MONKS.
HE WAS A GREAT PHILANTHROPIST IN THE NAME OF BUDDHISM.
ONE DAY, HE WENT TO SEE THE GREAT TEACHER **BODHIDHARMA.**
"BODHIDHARMA," HE ASKED, "WHAT MERIT IS THERE IN ALL OF MY GOOD WORKS?"
AND THE GREAT TEACHER BODHIDHARMA SAID, "NONE WHATSOEVER."

THEN EMPEROR WU ASKED, "WHAT IS THE PRIMAL MEANING OF HOLY REALITY?"
CREEAAK.
THE GREAT TEACHER BODHIDHARMA ANSWERED, "EMPTINESS, NOT HOLINESS."
STOOP.
FINALLY, THE EMPEROR ASKED, "WHO, THEN, IS THIS CONFRONTING ME?"
"I DO NOT KNOW," WAS BODHIDHARMA'S REPLY.
AND THE EMPEROR DID NOT UNDERSTAND.
bok.
SO THE GREAT TEACHER BODHIDHARMA LEFT THE EMPEROR'S KINGDOM.

RIVETING.
SO WHAT'S TH' ANSWER?

THAT'S, UH.
THAT'S NOT REALLY HOW YOU DO IT.
IT'S A KOAN, REAGAN.

YOU CAN'T THINK OF IT LIKE A LOGIC PUZZLE. THERE ISN'T ONE SINGL
REASON T
OH GOD, HERE WE GO.
YER LUCKY I BROUGHT MY ASIAN WITH ME, CUZ I AIN'T UP FER THIS INSCRUTABLE SHIT T'DAY.
wuk wuk.

RAY!
WHAT? BETCHA HE SCRUTES LIKE A CHAMP. S'ALL IN TH' EYES, YANNO.
AH SO.

YOU ARE BEYOND TOLERATING.
WOULDN'T DO IT IF YOU DIDN'T LOVE IT.
SMACK!
AND "SCRUTE" IS NOT EVEN A WORD.
I SAY IT IS.

ahem.
BEN, THIS IS SCIPIO.
WITH A C, NOTTA K. ROMAN.
hi.

NICE TO MEET YOU.
CALL HIM SCIP. SCIP IS FINE.
ALRIGHT.
BUT NOT SCIPPY. CUZ ONLY I GET T'CALL 'IM THAT.
YOU ABSOLUTELY DO NOT.
AIN'T HE SUMTHIN'?
WORKS THAT FUCKIN' KILT.
GETTIN' ME ALL PREOCCUPIED AN' WHUTNOT.
PERVERT.
ASK 'IM WHAT HE DOES, BEN.
SORRY, WHAT?
FOR A LIVING.
ASK 'IM.
JUST TOO DAMN CUTE.
IT'S NOT THAT STRANGE.

WHAT DO YOU DO, SCIP?
bodyguard.
I'M, UM, I'M A CLOSE-PROTECTION OFFICER.
BODYGUARD.
C'N YOU BELIEVE THAT SHIT? PEOPLE ARE SPOZED T'BE SCARED-A THIS GUY.
WITH TH' ZEN AND TH' CHICKEN.

I DON'T TAKE FLORA TO WORK WITH ME, YOU KNOW.
"FLORA."
GOD.

YOU KNOW WHAT I MEAN, RAY.
IT'S JUST A FORMAL SORTA THING, BEN.
I PUT IT ON, AND I LOOK LIKE A JERK. IT'S NINETY PERCENT OF THE JOB.
OH.
I'VE GOT SOME JERK SUNGLASSES, TOO.
IT'S NOT BAD WORK, REALLY.
THE FIRM USUALLY ONLY HIRES ARMY GUYS AND COPS, BUT I HAVE ELEVEN YEARS OF SAN SHOU.
THEY SAID THEY COULD MAKE AN EXCEPTION FOR ME.
AN' I'M SURE BEIN' A GIGANTIC BLACK MAN DON'T GOT NUTHIN' T'DO WITH IT.
gi-gan-tic.

OH JESUS CHRIST, AS IF YOU WOULD EVEN KNOW!
YER RIGHT. I'M LYIN,' IT'S TINY.
YOU HAVEN'T GOT THE FIRST IDEA WHAT "IT" IS, AND YOU ARE A LUNATIC.
all miniscule n' shit.
WHAT'S THIS?
WHAT'S WHAT?
THE ZIPPERED POCKET.
OH. IT'S JUST FOR THE DUST MASK.
KEEPS THE SCALE FROM SCRATCHIN' IT.
YOU WEAR A DUST MASK?
WELL, YEAH. IN THE SUMMER. OBVIOUSLY. DON'T YOU?
I'VE NEVER BEEN HERE IN THE SUMMER.
I THOUGHT MASKS WERE, YOU KNOW. FOR PEOPLE WHO CARE TOO MUCH.

UHM, NO.
NO, THEY'RE FOR PEOPLE WHO WANT TO BREATHE.
YOU REALLY DON'T HAVE A MASK?
EVERYONE'S GOT A MASK.
YOU SHOULD GET A MASK.

OKAY.
REALLY.
FER FUCK'S SAKE, SCIP, HE HE DON'T NEED ONE RIGHT THIS SECOND.

he might.
HE DON'T.
LOOK, IGNORE THIS PUSSY. YER FINE. JUST GET A GOOD MASK BEFORE SPRING, ALRIGHT?

uh.
YOU CAUGHT TH' BUS INTA TOWN, DIN'T YA?
YA 'MEMBER SEEIN' A GREAT BIG DITCH?
CUTS RIGHT THROUGH TH' CITY LIKE A GIANT BUTTCRACK?
THAT'S TH' PHOCAS.

IT'S A RIVER, OKAY? WAS A RIVER.
IT COULD BE A RIVER AGAIN, IN THEORY.
ITSA RIVER BED.
ALL TH' WATER'S BEHIND A DAM IN CALIFORNIA.
TWO NOW, ACTUALLY.
RUSTLE.
TWO?! SERIOUSLY?
OH, AT LEAST.
FLUMP.
fuckin' soybeans.
BUT YEAH, ANYWAY. WHEN IT GETS WARM HERE, REAL HOT N' DRY? DUST FROM TH' RIVERBED GETS IN THE AIR.
CRAP'LL EAT HOLES IN YER LUNGS.
CLIC.
AN' THIS SHIT IS KNOWN. IT IS A FACT.

YES. DEFINITELY. COMPLETELY.
SO YOU NEED A MASK, OKAY? **NO KIDDING.** HERE, YOU CAN HAVE ONE OF MINE.
wind 'im up, watch 'im go.

YOU KNOW HE DON'T HARDLY NEVER GO OUTSIDE, RIGHT?
KING STREET QUALIFIES AS OUTSIDE. AND IT'S SHORELINE. THE AIR DOWN THERE TURNS TO GRAVEL WHEN-

SLAM.

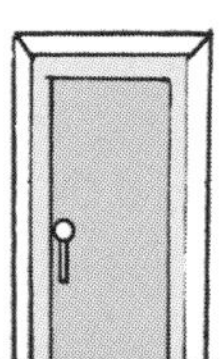

he, uh.
SO HE MIGHT. YOU KNOW. NEED STUFF.
LATER.
probably.
mm.

OKAY.
OH-KAY, SO I THINK THIS IS EVERYTHING.
YOU CAN KEEP IT.

THE FILTER NEEDS REPLACING, BUT THERE SHOULD BE SOME SPARES IN THE BAG.
FLATWORM BRAND. REALLY RELIABLE. THEY'RE LOCAL, SO THEY KNOW, Y'KNOW?
THANKS.
IT'S NOTHING. REALLY. I USUALLY JUST GIVE MY OLD MASKS AWAY TO A SHELTER, ANYWAY.
CUZ GOD FORBID TH' DOPE-SUCKERS DOWN IN SKINNER MOUTH-BREATHE THEIR FUCKIN' DOOM FIVE SECONDS AHEAD-A SCHEDULE.
I NEED A SMOKE.
WAIT, YOU'RE GOING?
need a smoke.
I CAN OPEN A WINDOW.
NO. NAH.
NAH, I GO BACK ON TH' CLOCK AT EIGHT. I BETTER SLEEP SOME.

IT'S STILL EARLY, THOUGH.
SO WALK ME OUT, THEN.
BEN?
I DON'T SMOKE.
START.
C'MON, LET'S GET GONE.
SCIP'S BUSY.
I'M NOT BUSY.
WE'LL DO SUMTHIN' THIS WEEKEND, OKAY? YOU AN' ME AN' BEN.
HERE Y'GO, KILLER.
ACT LIKE A WRITER.
uh.
oh my god, ray.

THAT IS ABSOLUTELY THE MOST EVIL THING I HAVE EVER SEEN YOU DO.
BULLSHIT. I ATE THAT PANDA.
THAT WAS NOT A PANDA AND YOU KNOW IT WAS NOT A PANDA.
I DUNNO. TASTED PRETTY CUTE.
THE BUTCHERS IN LITTLE CAIRO ARE VERY.
uh.
very dishonest people.
RAY, SHOULD I BE SEEING THAT?

CRUNCH.
DUST

NO.
NO YOU SHOULD NOT AT ALL.
aw god.

ZORA.
SWEETHEART.
WHAT THE FUCK.
HI.
I'M HOME NOW, OKAY?

oh, boy.
NO.
YOU HAVE SCHOOL.
i CAME HOME, THOUGH.
BEN HAS PICKLES.
YOU DON'T COME HOME THAT WAY.
YOU GO TO SCHOOL AN' YOU STAY THERE AN' LEARN AN' THEN DADDY COMES TO GET YOU.
YOU LEARN 'TIL THREE AN' YOU AN' DADDY COME HOME T'GETHER.
i GOT MY SHIRT!
DUSTY
ZORADYSIS, HONEY?
I THINK AUNTIE REAGAN IS MAYBE WORRIED YOU MIGHT GET IN TROUBLE.
AND DADDY, TOO.
AND MAYBE YOU SHOULDN'T WALK AROUND ALONE, EVER.
because people are so horrible.
AUNTIE REAGAN'S GUNNA SOCK HERSELF A KIN'R'GARDIN TEACHER WHO DON'T NOTICE WHEN SHE'S SHORT ONE GOD DAMN LITTLE GIRL.

MAYBE SHE DID?
MAYBE GENE GOT A CALL.
JEEZIS, YOU BETTER HOPE NOT.
BOY CAN'T EVEN SPELL "CUSTODY HEARING."
C'MON, YOU. BACK T'SCHOOL.

LOOKS LIKE I GOTTA GO MAKE A DAMN SCENE.
oooOoooh.
YEAH, YOU LIKE THAT, HUH.

WELL, YOU GOT A REAL TREAT COMIN', THEN.
CUZ I GOTTA THUNDERHEAD GOIN' AS IT FUCKIN' WELL IS.

GONNA GET SO MANY PANTS PISSED IN THIS ROUND AIN'T NOBODY GONNA BUG YOU AN' YER OLD MAN 'TIL YER IN GRAD SCHOOL.

HEH.
UH.
IT'S, UHM.
THAT WAS ZORA.
SORRY. SHE KINDA DOES WHAT SHE WANTS.
WE'VE MET.
SLAM.
OH. GENE, TOO?
MM-HM.
HA. ONE SORT OF EXPLAINS THE OTHER, HUH?
I GUESS SO.
UH...
IF YOU'RE HOME, YOU CAN USE A CHAIR.
TO BLOCK THE DOOR, I MEAN. KEEP HER OUT.
IF YOU WANTED TO.
THAT'S A GOOD IDEA, THANK YOU.
OH, NO PROBLEM!
THAT'S WHY THE LAST GUY LEFT. THE DOOR. AND ZORA.
SHE'S REALLY... INQUISITIVE? KIND OF A SNOOP. GETS INTO EVERYTHING.
YOU WOULD BE SURPRISED.
really.

OH YEAH, DEFINITELY.
I MEAN, SHE'S NOT A BAD KID OR ANYTHING.
IT'S JUST, Y'KNOW, YOU TURN AROUND, AND THERE SHE IS. WITH YOUR WALLET.
HEH. KINDA FUNNY, ACTUALLY.
NOT THAT ZORA STEALS. I WOULDN'T
I THINK.
I THINK I'M GONNA GO HOME.
MAKE SURE EVERYTHING'S OKAY.
CREAK.
OH.
OH, OKAY. YEAH, THAT'S A GOOD IDEA.
mnh.
IT WAS NICE MEETING YOU. I'LL BE NEXT DOOR IF—
RIGHT.
THANKS. BYE.
CLICK.

oh god.

oh my god
oh my
GOD.
CLIC.

oh my god PLEASE You have GOT to be KIDDING ME.
COME ON.
NO, COME ON.
DON'T DO THIS DON'T DO THIS DON'T
DO THIS-
CREAK!
THUMP.

CRNKL
hhh.
paranoid.

PARANOID.
PARANOID.

ffh.

SSKH.
THUNDERBIRD TRIBE
VINLAND PEMMICAN
VIKING FLAVORED CEREAL

THK.
RUSTLE!

HOLD
Wringer Pharma
5005 Summitview
Yakima, WA 9890
#7596031-000
KOWALS
238 McCorm
Yakima, WA
TAKE ONE TAB
AS DIRECTED
WARNING
ALCOHOL INTENSIFIES
100 mg TABL

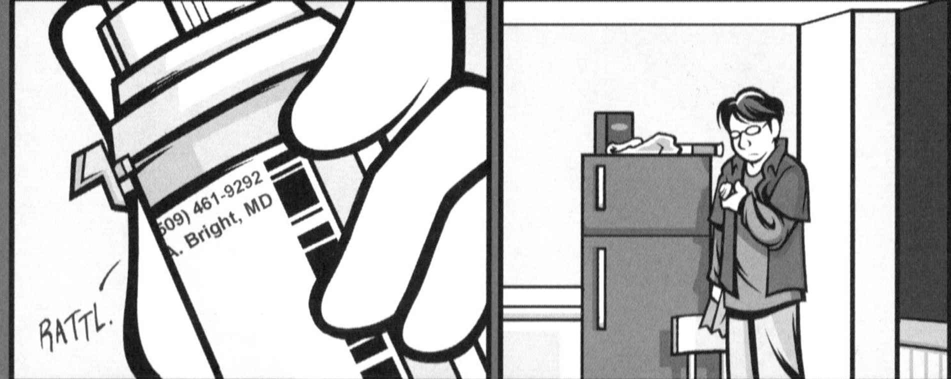

RING.

RING.

RING.
FINE UNFILTERED TOBACCO
BUZZ·BOMB
FLAVORED CIGARILLOS
VANILLA

RNNNCLIC.
SNIFF.

H'LO, YAKIMA VALLEY PSYCHIATRIC GROUP.
HI.
DOCTOR ALICE BRIGHT, PLEASE?

MMKAY SIR AN' WHO MAY I SAY IS CALLING PLEASE.
BEN.
BENJAMIN KOWALSKI.

MMKAY MISTER KOWALSKI PLEEZ HOLD AN' I WILL SEE IF DOCTOR BRIGHT IS AVAILABLE.
OKAY.
OKAY, THANK YOU.

CLIC.

HA.

YEAH, RIGHT.
HNH.

TSSST.
hm.
BEN!
TCH.

hi.
BEN?
HI.
IT'S ME.
DON'T HANG UP.

UH-OH.
HELLO?
YES, I'M HERE. EXCUSE ME. SORRY.
I'M SORRY, I YELLED. I DIDN'T MEAN TO YELL. I'M SORRY.
BEN, I NEED YOU TO TELL ME WHERE YOU ARE, PLEASE.

OH, UH.
NO?
NOWHERE.
I'M FINE.
WHAT'S HAPPENING? ARE YOU ALL RIGHT?

UH-HUH.
OKAY, WELL... GOOD.
THANK YOU FOR CALLING ME, BEN.
CAN WE TALK FOR A SECOND, NOW? BECAUSE THERE IS A LOT I NEED TO KNOW.

HEH.
YOU SOUND KINDA WEIRD.
MAYBE. I MIGHT.
I THINK I WOULD HAVE A GOOD REASON.
BEN, HAVE YOU CALLED YOUR PARENTS?
...
BEN?
HAVE YOU?
i want the confidentiality thing.
PHYSICIAN-PATIENT PRIVILEGE.
YEAH, THAT.
BEN-
DON'T TELL ANYONE I CALLED. REALLY.
IF I SAY YOU CAN'T, YOU CAN'T, RIGHT?
SO DON'T DO IT.
BEN, I WOULD NEVER SUGGEST YOU EVER DO ANYTHING I FELT WOULD BE DETRIMENTAL.
BUT IT HAS BEEN TWO MONTHS. YOUR MOTHER IS **WORRIED.**

SHE CALLS ME EVERY WEEK.
SHE'S VERY UPSET, AND THERE'S NOTHING I CAN SAY.
I LEFT A NOTE.
HA.
AW, BEN. C'MON. YOU'RE JUST TOO DAMNED SMART TO BELIEVE THAT'S ANYWHERE **NEAR** GOOD ENOUGH.
IT WAS A PRETTY GOOD NOTE.
OH, I DON'T DOUBT IT.
ARE YOU TAKING YOUR MEDS?
YEAH.
GOOD. THAT'S GOOD TO HEAR. I WANT YOU TO KEEP THAT UP.
YEAH.
BUT WE NEED TO CONSIDER REFILLS.
CLIC.
I **COULD** TRANSFER THE PRESCRIPTION TO A PHARMACY NEAR YOU.
BUT I GENUINELY DON'T FEEL COMFORTABLE MEDICATING ANYONE OUT OF MY DIRECT–
I DON'T NEED REFILLS.

...OKAY.
WHAT DOES
THAT MEAN.
HUMM
I HAVE
SIX
MONTHS
ALREADY.
WHAT?
IT'S FROM
WHEN DAD
RETIRED.
I WAS
GONNA
LOSE HIS
INSURANCE.
BLEET.

SO YOU WROTE
THE PRESCRIPTION
FOR TWICE A
DAY INSTEAD OF
DAILY.
I DID?
HEH.
YEAH.

HUH.
GUESS I
SHOULDN'TA
DONE THAT.
I DIDN'T
MIND.
CLIC
MM. SO, WHAT
HAPPENS IN
SIX MONTHS?
CLIC.
YOU'LL BE
BACK IN
SIX MONTHS?
um.

BEN.
I'M GOING TO TELL YOU WHAT I THINK.
I KNOW.
I THINK YOU NEED TO COME HOME. NOT IN SIX MONTHS. NOW.
I THINK YOU MADE A MISTAKE.
TEMPLAR -connect-
FEATURED
NEW
SKY VIKINGS AND THE THUNDERBIRD TRIBE •
Pretty Princess Raindrop is messily dispatched by Odin, and the Thunderbirds exact a terrible revenge! Join the battle, today after school!
IN THE COLISEUM •
No paternity tests. No court dates. No compromises. Claudius R. Graves is the only law. This episode: THUMBS DOWN.
KNIGHTS LACROSSE •
Three-day semi-finals begin!
NARROWBAND NEWS
CUZ YOU JUST DON'T WANNA HEAR IT.
Daily news briefs, available in:
- Liberal
- Conservative
- Ethnic
- Fringe
- Custom
- Good Only
- Bad Only
- Paranoid
- Inconsequential Prattle
MORE PROGRAMS
AND IT DISTURBS ME THAT YOU DIDN'T TELL ME YOU WERE THINKING ABOUT RUNNING AWAY. A LOT.
WE NEED TO TAKE CARE OF THIS.
DO YOU AGREE WITH ME?
CLIC CLIC CLIC CLIC CLIC
I GUESS.
TEMPLAR DAMAGE REPORT
LOCAL PROGRAMMING
MONDAYS WITH TUESDAY
LOCAL PROGRAMMING
THE FIELDS OF OSIRIS
LOCAL PROGRAMMING
Curious about Nile Revivalism?
VIRES ACQUIRIT EUNDO: TEMPLAR CIVIC INFORMA
LOCAL PROGRAMMING
Dust information, special events, city council
SUBSCRIBE
GOOD. THAT'S THE RIGHT DECISION.
I'M GENUINELY RELIEVED.
YEAH.

CAN YOU GET BACK ON YOUR OWN? DO YOU NEED HELP?
I'M FINE.
WHEN CAN WE EXPECT YOU?
WILL YOU CALL YOUR PARENTS?
CLIC.
IS THERE A NUMBER WHERE I CAN REACH YOU?
NO. NO, THIS ISN'T MY PHONE.
NO.
...OKAY. BEN, ARE YOU SAFE?
M'FINE.
ARE YOU SURE?
I'M **FINE**, EVERYTHING'S **FINE**. STOP **SAYING** IT THAT WAY.

I APOLOGIZE. I DIDN'T MEAN TO UPSET YOU.
YEAH.
YEAH, WELL.
CLINK.
that's good.
I WAS MAKING AN ASSUMPTION.
YOU DISAPPEARED FOR TWO MONTHS.
NO COMMUNICATION AT ALL.
LEFT A NOTE.
NO DIRECT COMMUNICATION.
AND THEN A CALL, OUT OF THE CLEAR BLUE SKY.
PICKL
I WAS WORRIED ABOUT THE MOTIVATION FOR IT.
NOTHING. IT'S NOTHING BAD.
IT'S JUST... I DUNNO.
I JUST HAD A GOOD DAY.
WANTED TO TELL SOMEONE.
AND THEY'D KNOW WHAT I MEAN.

FIN.

TEMPLAR, ARIZONA.

INTERMISSION:

the Sincerists.

oh, for god's sake.

VERITAS

WARNING
this is a
SINCERIST
ESTABLISHMENT.
DECEPTION STRICTLY PROHIBITED!!

YES, OKAY. I SEE YOU.

WHAT.

WHAT DO YOU WANT.

I'M ASKING YOU A QUESTION.

ANSWER. SAY SOMETHING.

POINT.

KASPER

...RIGHT.
Y'KNOW WHAT? YOU'RE GETTIN' COFFEE.
YOU LIKE COFFEE? THAT'S ENOUGH FOR A COFFEE.
I'M GETTIN' YOU A COFFEE. SMALL.
KASPER
fuckin' wickerheads.
SO, THE SYMPOSIUM IS ABOUT TO START.
THREE MINUTES FROM THE BELL.
AND BELLA TAKES OFF THE JACKET.
PINK BELLY SHIRT. WITH RHINESTONES.
SPELLING PRINCESS.
jesus.
YES. THIS FUCKIN' BIG.

SO WHAT HAPPENED?
WHAT DO YOU THINK? SIMONE POPPED HER IN HER STUPID GODDAM MOUTH.
THAT'S GOOD.
GOD. FUCKIN' POSER.
GOD.
SHOWS UP TO A SINCERIST SYMPOSIUM IN A SHIRT THAT IS A LIE.
GOD.
BUT SIMONE IS COOL, RIGHT?
ARE YOU KIDDING, SIMONE IS MY GOD.
THERE IS NOTHING MORE SINCERE THAN A PUNCH IN THE FACE.
SHE SHOULD BE OUR CHAPTER FUCKING PRESIDENT.
VERI

I MEAN, IT'S JUST...
ah.
'MEMBER WHEN PEOPLE CARED?
WHEN THIS THING WAS REAL?
LIKE WITH JOE.
JOE WITH THE TATTOO.
MM.
NOTICE
PLEASE MAINTAIN TRUTHFUL EXCHANGES AT ALL TIMES
- Mngmt
"COURAGE" IN CHINESE.
THERE WAS AN INQUISITION.
FIVE HOURS. NO BREAKS.
FINALLY BOOTED HIS ASS OUTTA TH' LOFTWALL CHAPTER WHEN HE ADMITTED HE HATED **PARROTS.**
AN' I JUST MEAN **NO HESITATION.** OUT.
WHAT TH' **FUCK**, YANNO? WHERE DID THAT **GO**?
MMN. YEAH.
YOUR DEDICATION T' **TRUTH CULTURE** IS REAL HEARTENING, HAZEL.

THANK YOU FOR YOUR HONESTY, ARTHUR.
NO, NO.
DON'T DISMISS. **CONSIDER.**
I'VE BEEN SINCERE FOR YEARS. EIGHT OR NINE.
AND I JUST DON'T **SEE** PEOPLE LIKE YOU. I'M SO PLEASED.
AR-THUR!
I'D PROBABLY FUCK YOU, BUT YOUR FACE IS ATROCIOUS.
AND THERE'S THAT ODOR.
DO YOU WASH?
...YES.
WOULD NOT HAVE GUESSED.
TH.
THANK YOU FOR YOUR HONESTY.
MM.
CAN YOU GET THE CHECK? I DON'T FEEL LIKE PAYING.
END

Footnotes.

Page 1

Let's get off to a weird start: Before page one ever saw the light of day, and long before the plot was set in stone, Ben was going to be blind.

Just throwing that out there.

Abandoned that idea, though. It just proved to be too impractical. And, dare I say, kinda cheesy.

Also, this is probably the structurally weakest comic page I've ever drawn.

Page 2

I am completely willing to admit that the Abusive Editor character is mind-numbingly cliché. But in my defense, he won't stay that way.

Ben's editor is named Andrew Pierce, which is a reference to Ambrose Bierce, another newspaper editor better known as the author of The Devil's Dictionary. They're both so cynical that they find it difficult to function, but Pierce doesn't have the excuse of a massive battlefield head wound to account for his terrible personality.

Page 3

Nudity by the third page. I'm one classy broad.

Ben sleeps naked. Everybody should.

Page 5

My favorite thing on this page is the woman in the *chador* and *niqab* with the eyebrow ring. I like to think that if we had a full-body shot of her, she'd be wearing black patent leather platform boots, too.

Page 6

If a comic page can be symbolic instead of narrative, this one definitely is. I kinda had it planned as something people could come back to two hundred pages in the future and understand all the references.

There's a guy putting on a dust mask, a woman in a Flatworm brand jacket, and an ancient Roman Pastime. Also visible is some of the decayed splendor of Ben's neighborhood, Riverside.

Page 7

Far off in the background we can barely see Loft's Wall, or Loftwall, or Loft's Folly. It was originally a Spanish battlement, but

but some over-rich cartel of ranchers had it imported over, brick by brick, back when that sort of thing was okay. I think Loft's Wall predates William Randolph Hearst turning an ancient Roman temple into a Californian swimming pool ornament, though, which is probably the best-known example.

Page 8

Sandwich of the Damned

- 2 Eggo waffles
- Lettuce
- Deli meat of choice
- Imitation maple syrup
- Horseradish

Toast waffles. Place thin bed of washed, patted-dry lettuce on one waffle, to avoid soaking waffle with meat juices. Pile on meat. (Pictured: Corned beef.) Garnish with imitation maple syrup and horseradish to taste.

Wash down with pickle brine.

Page 9

I hate thought balloons and I wish I never had to draw them.

When I'm forced to draw them, they're done with images or abstract symbols. Anything but full sentences. I mean c'mon, SHEESH. Who thinks in monologues?

Page 11

So Ben knows both Zora and Reagan at the beginning of the story, but we don't know how. Why? Because it's not important right now. But I'll get to it. Don't worry.

I made the name Zoradysis up. Google it if y'don't believe me. So if any of you guys name your kid that, I want royalties, understand?

Page 12

Hey, it's Gene! Hi, Gene!

It's barely noticeable, but Gene has rosacea. This is my favorite part about him.

He barely gets a nod this chapter, but I had a lot to do, ya know? Look for him in the future.

Page 14

Zora knows Daddy is stupid.

Page 16

Enter Reagan Mancuso. Fat lady, four-eyes, fan favorite, force of nature. When I offered commissions and sketches during the Pre-Order Project to pay the printing bill for this book, she was far and away the most requested subject.

Most of her wardrobe is inspired by drag

queen couture. I spend a lot of time on YouTube looking for references. John Waters movies are good, too.

Page 18

My first big, fat continuity error: There was a couch in Ben's front room which shouldn't have been there. His front room's too small for that. I corrected the problem in the print version, but you can still see the mistake online.

Page 21

Jumping on someone else's bed with your shoes on, and lighting up without asking.

First impressions are important.

Page 22

The chapter's first music references, not counting the chapter title. Clutch songs.

Page 23

The butt in the first panel was drawn from a reference image. I found the photo online, cropped almost exactly like that. I don't know who the butt belongs to, though.

As a result of perfect reference, I must say that this is a particularly magnificent and successful ass-drawing.

Page 26

And now we're downtown.

Templar has crows instead of pigeons. No real reason for it other than that's how I want it.

Stuffed in the background of the second panel, between the billboards for Templar's red-light district and some trashy television show, is about half of a building. It's loosely referenced from a site about the sort of heroic, overblown architecture Communist party leaders envisioned building in Moscow in the '30s and '40s, but never got around to. Google "Unrealized Moscow" for more.

In the second panel: Ads for clothing and makeup, Flatworm and Shiner brands respectively.

Page 27

My husband once witnessed a real-life bucket boy/bagpiper duet in Harvard Square in Cambridge, Massachusetts. He reports that it sounded pretty good. Wish I'd heard it.

The bucket boy is a very crude sort of half-portrait of William Elliott Whitmore, a man who makes music that I think you should buy.

Minerva's Shield is a real dish, by the way. It was served at ancient Roman banquets, where the obscurity of the ingredients in a recipe sometimes trumped the taste of the final results in importance.

Page 28

Lower right corner of the bottom panel.

That's a watermelon.

Someone has managed to heave an entire watermelon across a street at this guy. WOW. The person who just flung the crumpled-up paper ball must be feeling pretty lousy right now.

And did you notice the turd? I like the turd a lot. It makes me think. I mean, is that fresh, or was this planned? Who or what did it come out of? Is this a turd of opportunity, or is it part of a poo-tossing conspiracy? Is there more coming?

Page 29

More Pastimes. Ren-festers and historical re-enactors are good people. I'm glad they put so many photos online.

These two aren't being very good about their Pastiming, though. Stricter interpretations of the lifestyle disapprove of people who mimic different time periods hanging out together. The girl on the left is done up in some all-purpose Renaissance peasant garb. The one on the right is rockin' early Victorian era.

And I'm not even gonna touch how out-of-line eating fast food is.

Page 30

Yeah, Ben Kowalski. No, he's not biracial. I'll get to it later, but I'm willing to bet you guys can already hazard a guess.

But hey, you might ask, why doesn't Reagan, in her infinite rudeness, grill him about his anomalous surname? Answer: She already did when they first met.

Page 31

Ray is not a joiner.

And strictly speaking, those two Pastimes probably wouldn't "do Latin" at her. They're not hardline enough in their scene to bother learning any, and it wouldn't be historically accurate anyway.

Page 33

People love this page. They are right to love it. I love it, too.

Templar's slur on the honor of Jimmy Carter is strongly inspired by Horatio Greenough's 1840 sculpture of George Washington, the first statue ever commissioned by Congress. It depicts Washington naked to the waist, ripped like a Greek god, and wearing a loose toga. It is pretty ridiculous. The Smithsonian has it squirreled away in National Museum of American History in Washington, DC.

Page 34

This little story was important to me, because it sort of informs you guys that Templar isn't some circlejerk utopia. Stuff goes wrong and gets half-assed, just like everywhere else. Too many fictional cities either seem to be self-destructing dystopias or the author's idea of paradise. Those are both pretty boring after the umpteenth time you read about them.

Also on the page: Wickerheads.

Page 35

Reagan's quoting Mojo Nixon in that last panel. Words to live by.

Page 36

Jethro Tull reference, although I prefer Clutch's cover.

I talked smack about fictional utopias on the page 34 footnote, but Templar's full of places I wish were real. Clay bars are a prime example.

Page 37

Reagan's accent is founded in the traditional "Noo Yawk" mutilation of the English language, but it's got some weird uses of emphasis, tone, and antiquated slang thrown in for variety. The expression "get born" should have never gone out of style. It's so useful.

Page 40

I like this page because it manages to communicate an important fact about Ben while being entirely unhelpful about the details.

Page 42

I picked the three most tedious classics I've ever read for the bottom panel.

Page 43

This bar's owner has a shrine behind the counter to Bes, Osiris, and Sekhmet. Bes is the a god of pleasure and a household protector. Osiris is a god of resurrection, immortality, and fertility. Sekhmet is an avenging goddess whose warlust can only be placated by drinking vast quantities of beer mixed with pomegranate juice so that it resembles blood.

The bar's owner is a Nile Revivalist, and these are her favorite gods. A god of pleasure and a goddess who loves beer are sensible choices of worship for a barkeep, and Osiris... well, who doesn't like the idea of immortality?

Page 45

Like the zeal of the converted, the civic pride of the transplant can be pretty excessive. Ray's not from Templar, but it's her adopted hometown.

Page 46

I've had at least two or three people write me to tell me they planned on getting hip flasks engraved like Reagan's. One even came through with a photo, recently. Very cool.

Page 50

This is a real Buddhist koan.

Page 51

The standard clearance for modern interior doors in six feet, eight inches. Scipio's not quite that tall, but he's still tall enough that he instinctively hunches over to get through.

And this is the best comic page in the entire book. It's one of the few I can say turned out exactly how I wanted.

Page 52

Ben's not actually Japanese. Just so you know.

Page 54

"Scipio" is a real name. It's Latin for "ceremonial staff."

Back in the days following black American emancipation (in Templar's reality as well as our own), there was a fad among freed slaves to name their children after ancient Romans of historical note. It's been abandoned by most, but you catch echoes of it now and then in black men named things like Caesar or Augustus. Scipio's family never stopped doing this.

There are lots of Scipios in Rome's history. Templar's Scipio is named for Scipio Aemilianus Africanus, who besieged and ultimately razed Carthage during the Third Punic War.

Page 57

San Shou is a modern Chinese fighting system, with an emphasis on self-defense and combat efficiency. It can be pretty ugly, since it's not shy about choke holds, cheap shots, and joint locks. It's not for show.

Page 58

Scip isn't a ren-fest geek. Note that no one present thinks his scale mail is weird.

A lot of men's formal wear in general retains barely-perceptible nods to armor and/or military uniforms. In this Arizona, they're a lot less subtle.

The scale mail in his suit isn't a bulletproof vest, or functional in any way. It's probably made from aluminum. After all, your tux's cummerbund isn't there to hold your dueling pistol, right?

Crummier suit sets probably just have scale-patterned tunics, while nicer suits have engraved silver scales, enamel, or better.

Page 60

A crash course in Templar's unique meteorological situation. They're kind of like in a mini-Dustbowl.

Page 61

"Lungs like a gold/silver/silica miner" would be more accurate, but no one would have known what the hell I was talking about.

Silicosis. It's a bitch.

Page 63

Ray isn't usually this passive-aggressive. It's probably worth noting.

Page 68

Made-up slang in panel three. I'm kinda proud of it.

I've never heard anyone use the phrase "get a thunderhead going" to describe anger, but it seems very natural, and someone, SOMEWHERE has probably used it, which is a good sign. The problem with most invented slang is that it tries too hard. Ideally, I think you shouldn't even notice it.

Page 72

That's a fuse box Ben's opening under the sink. Terrible, possibly illegal place for it.

The building Ben and company live in wasn't designed as an apartment house; It was just rehabbed into one, and rather unevenly. As a result, room sizes and appointments vary in each apartment. For example, Scip has a huge living room. Ben's is hardly large enough to turn around in.

Page 74

"Viking flavor" is like soft mead, which is just spiced, diluted honey. There's also an Indian flavor, which is berry-based.

Vinland Pemmican cereal is part of the merchandising for the kiddie show "Sky Vikings and the Thunderbird Tribe," a cartoon about Vikings in flying longboats and Native Americans that ride enormous eagles. They fight. A lot.

Since it's inspired by a kiddie show, it's

obviously a kiddie cereal. I imagine it's cloyingly sweet. It's a little odd a guy Ben's age eats it, but not very.

Page 75

Ben's address isn't real, but McCormick Street in Yakima, Washington is.

Wringer Pharmacy isn't real either, But Summitview Avenue also exists, and this made-up address would be about 6 miles from the address listed on the prescription bottle.

Please don't dial that phone number. I don't know who you'll get, if anybody. I just couldn't bring myself to make it a 555 number to guarantee fakeness.

Page 77

That's a trilobite etched into Ben's laptop. It means his computer isn't very top-of-the-line. A nicer machine from the same manufacturer would feature something higher up the evolutionary ladder. He'd need at least a dimetrodon to play all the new games.

Page 80

A lot of readers hate Dr. Bright. Poor Dr. Bright.

Page 82

I hope you guys are taking notes. You might want to try this trick yourself, one day.

And a 21-year-old man with a retired father? Someone got a late start.

Page 83

Templar Connect is the local free (although I imagine they take out the difference in taxes) wireless DSL. Anyone with a computer, a Templar address, and a decent paper trail to prove it can get one.

This is probably the closest to sci-fi Templar's "otherness" will ever get. But it's really not that unusual. Sometime in the past, all personal computer monitors were TVs. Eventually, computers needed better support than a TV display could offer, so specialized monitors were made for 'em. The rest is history. For us, anyway. Where Ben lives, the TV people stepped up to the plate, and TVs and computers were never really separated. And the inevitable happened a lot sooner for them than it's happening for us. "Dumb" TVs still exist in Templar, and we'll eventually see 'em, but it's kinda like owning a turntable.

Page 86

Was that unsatisfying? Do you have any questions? God, I sure hope so.

Page 87

This comic's chapters are all going to be separated by these intermissions, because there's a lot to the city of Templar that doesn't directly involve the main cast. This first intermission was a test. I'm not one hundred percent thrilled with how it turned out, mostly because of the medium. I think I'm gonna stick to straight black-and-white inks (without toning) in the future.

Page 89

Wickerheads again.

Page 91

Yes, the Cafe Veritas will kick you out if they think you're lying in a private conversation and the waiters or cashier happen to hear you. This is what makes them a Sincerist cafe.

Hazel, like all scenesters, took it personally when the next generation of joiners didn't meet her expectations. Sincerism is about never ever lying EVER, and she's decided that involves more than what comes out of your mouth. Not everyone follows the same interpretation, but she enjoys complaining enough to make the ultra-fascist approach worth the trouble.

Page 92

Yeah, this was a five-page set-up for a cheap joke. Sue me.

Sincerism is stupid. It's built to spill. Lies are a necessary part of civil interpersonal communication, even when it's just telling your barista to have a great day when you really couldn't care less what happens to her after you get your latte. Honesty, like all virtues, is easy to take to unworkable extremes.

Hearing the unedited, uninvited truth about yourself — or rather, what the people you talk to consider to be true about you — is tough. Hearing it every day, for years on end, is impossible. it's safe to assume anyone who stays Sincerist for longer than it take to grow out of their Angry Teenager Phase is either too weak to shed the devil they know in favor of uncharted waters, or just a total fucking sadist.

And that's book one! We're just getting started, guys. Plenty more to read at http://www.templaraz.com.

Thanks.

Sketches.

SHE'LL
SHOW UP
LATER.

ALL OF
THIS STUFF
IS FROM
2001 OR
EARLIER.

FASTER
USSYCAT
L, KILL

I WAS GONNA LEAVE THIS OUT, BUT I FIGURE IT'S SO OLD AND SO MUCH HAS CHANGED SINCE THEN THAT IT DOESNT REALLY SPOIL ANYTHING.

SPIKE WAS BORN IN 1978
IN WASHINGTON, DC AND
GREW UP IN THE DC SUBURBS,
SHE CURRENTLY LIVES IN CHICAGO.